Forthcoming titles in this series will include

- *Winning Negotiation Tactics!*
- *Basic Business Finance!*
- *Successful Business Planning!*
- *Winning CVs!*
- *Getting Hired!*
- *Managing People for the First Time!*
- *Successful Interviewing Techniques!*
- *Letter Writing for Winners!*
- *Winning Telephone Techniques!*

Do you have ideas for subjects which could be included in this exciting and innovative series? Could your company benefit from close involvement with a forthcoming title?

Please write to David Grant Publishing Limited
80 Ridgeway, Pembury, Tunbridge Wells, Kent TN2 4EZ
with your ideas or suggestions.

BECOME
ASSERTIVE

!

James Fleming

60 Minutes Success Skills Series

First published 1997 by
David Grant Publishing Limited
80 Ridgeway, Pembury, Kent TN2 4EZ United Kingdom

60 Minutes Success Skills Series is an imprint of
David Grant Publishing Limited

British Library Cataloguing in Publication Data
A CIP catalogue record for this book is available from the British Library

ISBN 1-901306-01-1

Cover design: Steve Haynes

Text design: Graham Rich

Production editor: Paul Stringer

Typeset in Futura by
Archetype, Stow-on-the-Wold
http://ourworld/compuserve.com/homepages/Archetype

Printed and bound in Great Britain by
T.J. International, Padstow, Cornwall

This book is printed on acid-free paper

CONTENTS

WELCOME!

ABOUT *BECOME ASSERTIVE!*

This book is part of the 60 Minutes Success Skills Series. Can you learn to stop being a doormat and assert yourself in just one hour? The answer is a resounding "Yes".

The only bit of waffle in the book

The 60 Minutes Series is written for people with neither the time nor patience to trawl through acres of jargon, management-speak and page-filling waffle. Many people would have you believe that assertiveness is part of your personality – if you've got it, fine; if not, tough luck. This is nonsense. Assertiveness is a skill that can be learnt, like riding a bike, only easier. And it can be picked up quickly.

This book recognises that time is precious. Like all the books in the series, we believe that you can learn all you really need to know quickly and without fuss. Our aim is to distil the essential, practical advice you can use straight away.

Is this book for me?

Being assertive does not mean being aggressive, nor does it mean bottling things up. Assertive people tend to be:

○ *less stressed;*
○ *more confident;*
○ *good at dealing with others;*
○ *better members of a team.*

Become Assertive! is for anyone who would like to make more of an impact, and take greater control of their own lives. Assertiveness is a very positive asset. Being assertive means feeling good about yourself and looking after your own interests as well as those of others. It is about having a say in the direction you are taking rather than being at someone else's beck and call. It is also about being more self-confident, standing up for your own point of view, valuing your own judgements. People with assertiveness skills can:

○ *present their views more confidently – and have their voices heard;*
○ *deal more effectively with aggressive people;*
○ *get things done their way and earn greater respect.*

This book is certainly for you if you find that:

○ *people always seem to "walk all over you";*
○ *your ideas are seldom heard;*
○ *you find it difficult to deal with bullies (be it the boss, colleagues, neighbours or members of the family);*
○ *you always go along with others – anything for a "quiet life";*
○ *you always shy away from conflict situations;*
○ *you put up with sub-standard service*

Does any of this feel familiar? If so this quick, no-bull guide to being assertive is just what you need. Read on.

How to use this book

The message in this book is "It's OK to skim". You don't have to read it all at once, or follow every tip to the letter. *Become Assertive!* has been written to dip into, so feel free to flick through to find the help you most need. It is a collection of hands-on tips that will help you stand up for your rights in a more positive way. In just 60 minutes, you can learn the skills you need to make a bigger impact on those around you. The only question that remains is whether the world is ready for the new you!

You will find that there are graphic features used throughout the book.

This means "Something to think about" – it sets the scene and identifies the problems by prompting you to think about situations which will instantly feel familiar.

With the problem diagnosed, these features give you an action plan – this will help you to get your own ideas in order.

This feature appears at the end of each chapter. It is a checklist which condenses all of the advice given throughout the chapter. Similar features appear within chapters which are overflowing with tips!

As you read through the book, you will come across lots of practical advice. But, if you're really pushed for time, you can always flick to the tips feature at the ends of chapters – these are also a useful reminder when you come back to look at this book in the future.

Good luck!

What's in this chapter for you

What being assertive means to you
How assertive are you now?
What assertiveness is not
Why learn to become more assertive?
Knowing aggressive behaviour when you see it
Ten basic assertiveness skills

> ❝ *I used to think that being assertive meant being more aggressive.* ❞
> **– Dave Shenberg, buyer**

This is a common mistake to make. "Assertion" and "aggression" sound similar, and are often confused. Yet they could not be more different.

> Think of people you know who are assertive. What makes you think of them as assertive?

What being assertive means to you

> ❝ *Now I see that being assertive means standing up for myself and being more self-confident – it doesn't mean rubbing people up the wrong way.* ❞
> **– Dave Shenberg**

Being assertive is all about self-worth. It's about making your own views clear and your voice heard. But it does not mean doing things at other people's expense. You do not need to be pushy, aggressive, or a bully to be assertive. Assertiveness is not about "I win, you lose". It's about "I win, but you win too" (or at very least the other person doesn't lose out). Assertiveness involves negotiating terms that you and others find acceptable. This means standing up for yourself without losing your temper, putting the other person down, or making them feel that they have lost in some way.

Use time as an ally.

❑ *Don't be dragooned into giving an instant response to a request. Buy time. Say: "I'm not sure about this – please give me some time to think it over and I'll get back to you very soon". This gives you a chance to gather your thoughts, true feelings and arguments.*
❑ *If someone is being very aggressive towards you, say the most honest thing you can, but calmly and politely. Try this: "I can see that you're very agitated at the moment – let's talk later".*

How assertive are you now?

> **❝** *A bit of self-analysis is always a good starting point.* **❞**
> **– Red Pearson, trainer**

How assertive are you? To answer this question, you have to be honest with yourself and perhaps accept that you have hang-ups. Most of us do.

Take a few moments to look at these statements. Write a number from 1 to 5 beside each one to show how appropriate they are to you – the scale is: 1 = no way, José, 2 = not really, 3 = sometimes, 4 = fairly often, and 5 = yep, that's me.

I find it embarrassing when people pay me a compliment ___

I hate telling other people they are wrong ___

I feel that other people take advantage of me ___

I would rather have a quiet life than stand up for myself ___

I am afraid to argue with the boss or people in authority ___

I do not speak out in meetings ___

I feel slighted or overlooked ___

Add up your scores. If yours was over 20, the chances are that you could certainly benefit from being more assertive. And remember, it is something you can learn to do. Look again at the statements – by learning assertiveness, you also learn to:

○ *accept compliments (and criticism);*
○ *tell people bad things about themselves;*
○ *express your opinions and have them respected;*
○ *stand up to the boss without being aggressive;*
○ *feel more of an equal partner with your colleagues.*

Take a typical "problem" situation and imagine how you could act differently.

❑ *If you find something very difficult to say, be honest. Start with: "I'm finding this very hard to say, so you'll have to excuse me, but . . ."*
❑ *If you always feel the victim in life, tell yourself that this is all part of your passive character. Recognise that this can change with practise.*

Assertiveness – what it's not

Let's now bury some of the misconceptions about being assertive.

> **❝** *I used to think that being aggressive at work was the only way to get things done. This of course led to a very unpleasant atmosphere in the office. We were never a team. Everyone tried to outdo each other and there was a lot of backbiting. Yes, you got things done by being aggressive, but it's no way to build good teamwork, or a good relationship with customers.* **❞**
> **– Red Pearson**

Assertiveness is nothing to do with being aggressive. Agression involves:

○ *doing other people down;*
○ *being a winner while other people lose;*
○ *ignoring the wishes of others;*
○ *getting annoyed and losing your temper;*
○ *being selfish.*

It's also nothing to do with being passive, which involves:

○ *being eager to please others all the time;*
○ *being unwilling ever to say "no";*
○ *always apologising for your actions;*
○ *always thinking other people must be right, and you wrong;*
○ *usually hiding your own feelings.*

Does any of this sound familiar?

> ❝ *I used to be really passive at work. I would never say 'no' to even the most unreasonable request. I hated letting people down and, I suppose, worked extra hard to make people like me. The result of all this passive behaviour was overwork, a constant feeling of self-pity and worthlessness. I also felt that everybody was against me and that the world was such an unfair place.* ❞
> **– Jan Capple, financial officer**

Jan Capple's experience is very typical of non-assertive people. There's that constant "put upon" feeling. In an attempt to make everyone else happy, they make themselves feel insecure, hard done-by, and often suffer feelings of guilt.

> **Do you *really* believe that non-assertive people can change? Belief is the first step – work at convincing yourself that you CAN become more assertive.**

Assertiveness is a skill, like driving or riding a bike – once you know how to do it, it's easy.

To begin with, try these simple techniques:

❑ *Avoid making snap decisions. If someone is in a hurry for your assistance, take at least 30 seconds to think of the reply you'd like to give.*
❑ *Think of what YOU want and be eager to please yourself as well as others.*

Why learn to become more assertive?

There are lots of good reasons. This is Jan Capple's experience.

❝ *Since doing some assertiveness training, my life is measurably better. I am more effective at work, both in what I do and the relationships I have with others. I am a much better team member.*❞

Being assertive will help you become:

○ *more effective at work and better at working with others;*
○ *better at dealing with irate customers or colleagues (or, even, members of your family);*
○ *more relaxed and have more energy;*
○ *more honest with yourself and with others;*
○ *more able to deal with difficult situations;*
○ *better at delegating and saying "no" to unreasonable requests;*
○ *better able to criticise others more constructively.*

Think of all the good reasons why you should become more assertive. Keep them at the front of your mind to spur you into action.

Remember, being assertive means taking control of your life but *not* at the expense of others. We'll see more in the following chapters.

There's no reason not to start right away.

- ❑ *Pick a day when you are going to start becoming more assertive. Think of this as a New Year's resolution that you really intend to keep this time. Try to do at least one assertive thing each day.*
- ❑ *Tell people that you have decided to become more assertive and tell them why you are doing it.*

Knowing aggressive behaviour when you see it

> ❝ *Once you've recognised what you and others are doing, it is easier to deal with it. Being a bit of an amateur psychologist can be useful.* ❞
> **– Dave Shenberg**

If you can recognise aggressive or passive behaviour in yourself, or in others, you will be better able to deal with it. You will find out in more detail how to cope with aggression or passivity later in the book. Meanwhile, here are some pointers to recognising aggressive signs in others, often an early hurdle for the assertiveness seeker:

- ○ *Watch out for the person who always uses "I" and "me". Self-centredness is a common sign of an aggressive personality. Aggressive people are usually poor listeners. The world revolves around them.*
- ○ *People acting as the self-proclaimed expert: "That'll never work"; "Nobody will agree to this"; "They'll never believe this".*
- ○ *Self-advancing statements, such as "Well, my customers never do this" or "It's never happened to me".*
- ○ *"Or else" statements – threats (often implied rather than openly stated). For example: "You must sort this out by tomorrow"; "You ought to get that done by tonight"; or "You'd better get on with it then".*
- ○ *Blaming others and events for failures.*
- ○ *Sarcasm as an alternative to discussion – "Yes, give us the benefit of your wonderful idea!"*
- ○ *Superiority – "I can't believe you did that!" "You must be joking, surely!" "Well, that's something I'd never do!"*
- ○ *An angry statement as an opener – "Are you mad!? Why did you do it!?"; "What the hell is happening there!?"*

If you're faced with an aggressive person, try to stay calm.

- ❑ *When someone tries to blame you unfairly, say something like: "Trying to blame people isn't going to resolve this situation is it?"*
- ❑ *Don't rise to a sarcastic comment. Best thing is not to visibly react at all.*
- ❑ *If you find that someone is being offensive, say so: "I have to say that I find that comment rather offensive/upsetting. I'd like to try to be more constructive."*

Ten basic assertiveness skills

As you begin to hone your assertiveness skills, remember:

1. Buy time before saying "yes" to any request. Think first: do you *really* want to do it?
2. Deflect aggressive comment. Try saying: "Let's talk later when you've calmed down a bit."
3. Be honest about your feelings – if you find something hard to say, own up. Say: "I find this quite difficult to tell you but . . ."
4. Break out of your victim mentality and tell yourself to take more control – you *can* do it!
5. Stop apologising for your thoughts and actions – people will respect you more.
6. Pick a date on which the new more assertive you will begin to emerge.
7. Watch for aggressive, self-centred people. If they keep saying "I", try saying, "Perhaps you'd now like to hear my point of view – it's worth waiting for!".
8. Don't let people get away with blaming you or others. Remind them that assigning blame rarely does any good.
9. Never try to counteract a sarcastic comment – remember it's come from a poor soul who still doesn't understand what assertiveness is all about. Turn the conversation around to something more positive.
10. Don't get caught in a tit-for-tat argument. But don't ignore it either. Say something like, "OK, how are we going to move this issue forward?"

Now that you know more about the difference between assertive, passive and aggressive behaviour, you will be better able to diffuse aggression or help other people become less passive. If you recognise passive or aggressive behaviour in yourself, you'll be better able to do something about it. Read on.

What's in this chapter for you

> *Your right to have rights*
> *Your right to be heard*
> *Your right to make mistakes*
> *Your right not to be overlooked*
> *How to assert your rights*

Your right to have rights

❝ *One of the things to watch out for as you become more assertive is the response of other people. For me, it was as if suddenly people noticed me. I woke up to find that for the first time people were listening to what I said and taking notice of my opinions. It was a bit scary at first, I can tell you.* ❞
– Gerry Pearson, junior retail manager

We are all used to having certain formal "rights". Examples include:

○ *the right to liberty and pursuit of happiness;*
○ *the right of free speech;*
○ *the right to be protected by the law;*
○ *the right to peace and security (hopefully).*

These are all rights bestowed by society. But many people are less clear about their own rights as human beings. Think of rights as a yardstick against which all kinds of behaviour are measured. Does the barman have the right to ignore you and serve his friends first? Do you have the right to attract said barman's attention by grabbing his tie? No – but you have the right to be heard and the barman has the right to politeness from customers.

But, if you are not certain that you have a right to be heard, for instance, how can you know when to act assertively? Similarly, other people have a right to be treated with respect, courtesy and understanding. No one has (or should have) the right to bully, threaten or force other human beings to do something against their will.

Here are some more basic human rights. They are rights that everyone should share. The right:

○ *not to be overpowered, abused, or made to feel small;*
○ *to make mistakes;*
○ *to be respected for who you are and the views you hold;*
○ *to ask for what you want, and make your own decisions;*
○ *to be fairly judged;*
○ *decide whether to be responsible for other people's problems*
○ *to do well.*

Think about which rights you generally lose out on. Do you fail to accept that they **are** your rights and that you should stand up for them?

Knowing that you have the right to have rights is the starting point to becoming more assertive.

> ❝ *Non-assertive people tend to think that only other people have rights . . . that only the other person has a right to decide or a right to get things done their way. This is wrong. Being assertive means you assert your rights – without infringing the rights of others.* ❞
> **– Dr Fran Barker, counsellor**

You could also think of your rights as basic freedoms – the freedom to act as you choose (without hurting others), the freedom to be more open and honest with others. Assertiveness aims to give you more freedom. Once you know your rights, you will at least be able to tell when other people are stepping over the mark.

Being able to recognise your rights is very important because every situation is different. Even people who are generally assertive may at times be unsure of themselves. Aggressive people aren't usually aggressive in *every* situation. The trick is to have a clear view of your rights as a person and judge each occasion on its merits. Keep asking yourself: "Do they have a right to say or do this to me?" "Do I have the right to be heard on this issue?"

Whenever you think "what right has he/she to speak to me like that?" remind yourself about your own right. You can always say: "I have a right to be treated properly" or "I have a right to reply to you."

Practise assertive responses so that they come to you naturally. Here are some useful ones which, of course, should be adapted to suit the occasion:

- *"I find those comments rather hurtful – maybe you would like to think again."*
- *"I would like the right to be heard here."*
- *"Please give me time to express my own views about this."*
- *"I am not happy about this. These are my views on the subject . . . please hear me out."*

Your right to be heard

❝ *There was a time when I was afraid to speak up in meetings or team sessions. Looking back, my hesitation wasn't shyness or nerves, it was more fundamental than that. I actually felt that I shouldn't say anything. I was new in the organisation, I was relatively inexperienced and much younger than the others. In truth, I thought I didn't really have the right to speak.* ❞
– Gerry Pearson.

Sound familiar? We are all sometimes hesitant to speak up for ourselves because we are not sure where we stand. It's common to think: "Do I have the right to say or do these things?"

Think about a recent time when you felt you hadn't been assertive enough. It could be at work (saying "yes" to a task that you knew you shouldn't have to do), in the family (giving in on some argument with your kids), in the shops or garage (accepting second-rate service). To what extent was it due to not knowing your rights?

❝ *I remember once taking a pair of faulty shoes back to the shop. Even though I had just bought them the day before, the manager fobbed me off with some excuse about not accepting liability. I wasn't sure where I stood legally, so I stayed silent. It's been annoying me ever since – I should have stuck to my guns.* ❞
– Fran Barker

Doing a bit of research always pays dividends. It clarifies the rights and wrongs and gives you a foundation for action.

Read about your rights as a consumer, as an employer or employee, as a citizen, as a parent, tenant, houseowner, taxpayer etc. The more you know about your rights, the more confident you'll feel about being assertive.

Once you have a clear understanding of your rights, you will feel more confident about speaking out, about being heard.

Remember, it is your right to be heard.

❑ *If in doubt about your rights, you have two options. (1) Ask the other person: "Could you explain my rights as a customer (etc.)?" Observe the response – you may find the other person starting to argue your case for you. (2) Bluff a little, but make sure you have a few good "get out" clauses. Try this: "I'm sure you'll find that under the law I have a right to a refund." Or: "I think I'm correct in saying that you don't have the right to do this." At the very least, this will buy you some time to gather your thoughts.*
❑ *Being thoroughly honest can be effective. You could, for instance, say: "I hear what you say but I'm not really sure about my rights on this issue. Let me do some research and come back to you. Maybe then we can come to a solution that is fair and satisfactory for both of us."*

The more confident you are about your rights, the easier it will be to make yourself heard. Being unclear about rights tends to make people nervous about saying anything in case they are wrong.

Your right to make mistakes

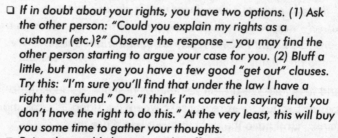

❝ *Everyone's got the right to get things wrong now and then.* ❞
– Flat Earth Society

Once you understand this very basic human right, life can become much less stressful.

> **How often do you feel afraid of doing the wrong thing at work? Does this fear inhibit you from being more assertive?**

For many people the fear of failure (or perceived failure at least) is enough to turn them into cowering wallflowers. Does any of this sound familiar?

- ○ *"I have strong views but I like to keep them to myself in case I'm wrong."*
- ○ *"I like to give the impression that I'm always in the right. One way to do this is never to stick my neck out."*
- ○ *"Speaking up for myself isn't worth the hassle if I get it wrong. I like the quiet life."*

The trouble with the "quiet life" is that it can often be a very resentful and bitter life too.

> **How many people do you know who have turned into resentful, cynical and rather bitter employees? This is often because they have spent all their working lives being ignored.**

Making mistakes can be beneficial. Many of the great advances in science, technology and medicine have come about because someone has made a mistake. We can learn from our mistakes. Organisations, too, learn from mistakes. Mistakes are often vital stepping stones to the right answer.

Knowing that you have the basic human right to make mistakes should encourage you to feel more confident about standing up for your views. And, if you're wrong? Remind people that being wrong is your right. Remind them that Columbus got his world view so wrong that he discovered America!

Work on believing in your right to be wrong.

- ❏ *Practise saying to yourself: "OK, I may be proved wrong but I'm going to give my opinions anyway."*
- ❏ *Another good thing to say to yourself and others is: "Being wrong is a risk we all take in our lives. I have as much right to be wrong as any man or woman."*
- ❏ *Stop feeling guilty about your views. Being wrong is nothing to be ashamed of. Admit to your mistakes straight away and you'll be surprised how forgiving others can be.*

Your right not to be overlooked

❝ *It doesn't matter how lowly you are in the organisation, you have a right to be taken into account. Sometimes, senior managers need reminding about this. We shouldn't always be passive and wait to be recognised for what we do and who we are.* ❞
– Rosa Maples, retail assistant.

"Our most important asset is our people". This phrase can be found screaming from the pages of many a mission statement. Yet many senior managers in organisations still ignore their subordinates.

Have you ever felt overlooked, passed by, ignored by colleagues or senior management. Looking back, what should you have said or done?

Being assertive means that you are confident enough to make your presence felt. The trick is to make it difficult for people to overlook you. This isn't a matter of being loud, aggressive or attention-seeking. It's about being visible, standing up for your ideas and beliefs, reminding yourself that you have as much right to be heard as any person.

Here are some tips on how to get noticed.

- ❑ *Build a reputation as a person to come to for advice and assistance. Send a memo round reminding people that they can come to you if they have any problems with, for example, new software, the new photocopier, office procedures, writing letters in French, or whatever your area of expertise.*
- ❑ *Make sure you always speak at meetings, even if it's just to support somebody else's point. However, don't overdo it. Develop a reputation as someone who is worth listening to.*
- ❑ *If you have done some work of which you are proud, discuss it with your senior manager. Never conceal or underestimate your achievements but don't appear boastful either. Make sure you get the credit for what you do.*
- ❑ *If a new job or task is coming up that you would like to be considered for, prepare a short note and send it to the relevant person – a senior manager or customer. Say that you would be happy to be considered for the job and state why you think you are the person who should be chosen.*
- ❑ *If you are overlooked for any reason, make it clear that you are disappointed. You can do this in person or in writing – just make sure that the other people know you were expecting to be considered. Maybe next time they will take you more seriously.*

The overriding message here is: don't just sit there and fume, act.

How to assert your rights

Knowing your rights is the key to assertiveness.

1. Sort out in your own mind what rights you think you have, whether at work or at home.
2. Remember that your primary right is to be treated with respect – at all times. It's other people's right too, so you must respect it.
3. Practise some key assertive responses: "You seem very upset – can we talk later?" "I would like the right to be heard here." "I'm not happy about this – I feel . . ."

4. Ask others to explain your rights as *they* see them. This can be an effective way to negotiate a constructive solution.

5. Don't accept it when somebody tells you that you have no rights in a certain situation – buy some time by saying you'll do some research and come back with the answer.

6. Remember that you have a human right to make mistakes. Don't put up with being made to feel small just because something has gone wrong – mistakes are a fact life.

7. If anyone criticises you for being wrong, remind them that even they have made mistakes, that you will learn from the error and that it should not be a question of personal insult or abuse.

8. Become indispensable by building up some expertise in a particular field so that people will come to you for advice and assistance.

9. Ensure you are recognised for your achievements by publicising what you have done. But, *never* boast.

10. If someone has let you down, make sure you tell them how disappointed, upset or frustrated you are. Do it in a way that respects their rights and you'll hammer home your point.

What's in this chapter for you

Your assertive "to do" list
Asking for things assertively
From apathy to empathy
Being an assertive customer
Assertive talk
Ten easy ways to become more assertive

> ❝ *Becoming more assertive isn't just a matter of making a new resolution and then hoping for the best. Like any skill, it helps if you have a strategy for picking up the key things you need to learn.* ❞
> **– Bob Fender, training planner**

This chapter looks at the various steps you need to take to become more assertive. Roll up your sleeves and get ready for action.

Your assertive "to do" list

> ❝ *I find it's very useful to start off with a personal 'to do' list. It must be practical, with some realistic goals and dates set aside. But, above all, it should not be too ambitious.* ❞
> **– Bob Fender**

How much do you really want to become more assertive? For many people, it's a daunting task and you'll need to be fully committed. But, once you start to see the benefits, you'll see the path to a more rewarding life.

Being assertive is not an innate trait of your personality. It is something you can learn, like language or any other communication skill. But where do you begin? A step-by-step "to do" list is a good start.

Here's an example "to do" list

(1) Make sure you really do want to change. Discuss the issues with friends and relations.

(2) Identify and list the situations in which you want to be more assertive: working in the office; meetings with customers, suppliers or subordinates; dealing with your bosses; handling domestic disputes; getting what you want from shops and restaurants, etc.

(3) Begin with three or four from your list. Start with those situations you think of as least threatening.

> *I decided last year to become more assertive in three areas: taking my car to the garage for a service, dealing with my teenage son and the weekly staff meetings at work. There are other areas which are more scary (such as my annual assessment) but I'm leaving those until I've become more confident. The least threatening of three on my list was the garage – then the meetings, then my son.*
> **(Dawn Ryder, teacher)**

Think of three or four scenarios in which you would like to be more assertive and jot them down. Leave out anything really daunting for the time being.

- ❑
- ❑
- ❑
- ❑

---

(4) Tell yourself that you are to be valued – that you **count**.

(5) Learn to carry yourself more assertively. This is often a good way to begin. Stand tall, push your shoulders back and keep your head straight. Get into the habit of looking people in the eyes as you speak. Learn to smile as you speak. Talk slowly and deliberately, as if every word you say is valuable.

(6)   Tell yourself that not everything you say or do needs to be popular. We all want to be liked by others, but sometimes we have to settle for being respected rather than popular.

(7)   Practise saying things in an assertive way:

"Thanks for that compliment, I really appreciate it."
"I want to be honest about your work. I hope you will hear me out."
"I don't feel happy with the work I've been doing. I would appreciate it if you could . . ."
"I really cannot agree to this situation. I would like you to give me some time to consider my response."

Say them in front of a mirror, while driving, or whenever you can. You will, of course, have to adapt your statements to the particular situations you have chosen, bearing in mind that you must respect the views of others.

Remember, assertiveness is not about win and lose, or lose and lose. The aim is to achieve a "win–win" situation for both sides.

Asking for things assertively

> ❝ *The way we ask for things often determines whether or not we are going to get what we want. If you ask for something with an apologetic, timid voice, it's like saying 'don't take this request too seriously' or 'I'm going to make it really easy for you to say no'.* ❞
> **– Don Harris, engineer**

Do you often find it difficult to ask for things – perhaps a favour at work, or help with a task? Think of the last time you felt unable to ask for help. Why did you chicken out?

The way you ask for things differs according to who you are asking. Asking a favour from a friend is easier than making a request to an aloof boss.

The first thing to do is to analyse why you find it so difficult to make requests of others.

- *"I hate to be refused, it's so embarrassing."*
- *"Asking for things shows how little I know – it puts me in the wrong."*
- *"I hate taking up other people's time."*
- *"It's not my place to ask for things."*

If any or all of these doubts are in your mind when you make a request you are bound to sound apologetic, weak, half-hearted and as if it's really OK to refuse.

If you need something, ask for it in the right way.

- ❑ *Before making any request tell yourself "I have the right to ask this". However, remember that the other person might have an equal right to refuse.*
- ❑ *When making a request, take an assertive (but not aggressive) stance and look at the person in the eye.*
- ❑ *Never start with an apology (for example, "I'm really sorry to ask this, but . . . ").*
- ❑ *Get straight to the point. Make your request short and snappy – don't try to soften up the other person with lots of irrelevant and trivial chat.*
- ❑ *Don't try to fawn your way into the other person's good books.*
- ❑ *If the request seems to be a little unusual, give an explanation of why you are making it now – and keep it short.*
- ❑ *Although it isn't always easy, try not to take a refusal as a personal slight. Keep the conversation (or correspondence) polite. Try to understand why the other person has refused your request. Seeing things from the other person's point of view is an essential part of becoming more assertive.*

Here are some useful "don'ts".

- *Never grovel or plead – you can't be assertive and subservient.*
- *Never get angry when refused a request – aggression is not assertiveness.*
- *Never sulk if the answer is "no" – work out why the request was refused and plan more carefully what to do next.*

> Watch out for aggressive or passive behaviour.
>
> ❑ *If the other person tries to drag you into irrelevant arguments, show that you appreciate his or her point of view but keep trying to repeat the core of the request. Try something like this: "I understand what you are saying but I'd really appreciate it if you could . . . [your request, again]."*
> ❑ *Always have a fall back position if the request is refused. What is your second-best outcome?*

If you're faced with an aggressive response, stay as cool as possible:

○ *"I really don't think you should get angry."*
○ *"I **do** have a right to make that request."*
○ *"Trying to make me feel guilty isn't going to sort this out."*

If you can maintain an air of quiet dignity and authority, you will be making the most powerful case for your request.

From apathy to empathy

❝ *Understanding the other person's point of view is half the battle in becoming more assertive.* ❞
– Fiona Craig, accounts manager

One of the main differences between assertiveness and aggressiveness is that the former takes account of the other person. Assertiveness is not a battle for supremacy, it is (or should be) about two equals. Empathy is the ability to feel as though you are in somebody else's place, to see things from their point of view. Empathising with the other person doesn't mean you cannot be assertive – in fact it's the other way round: to be assertive, you must have empathy with others. Here are some typical empathetic yet assertive statements and requests:

○ *"I know how you must be feeling, but this is why it needs to be done . . ."*
○ *"Of course I understand why you can't finish the job by tomorrow, but could I have a working version to present to the meeting by Friday?"*

○ *"I can see that you are very busy but I think it's in both of our interests to get that done."*

Having empathy helps to establish a rapport with the other person. It also helps in explaining the reasons for your request. The more you respect the other person, the more likely it is that he or she will agree to do what you ask.

Empathy is also a good ally in diffusing potentially aggressive situations. By understanding the other person's concerns and doubts, you can go half way to finding a solution that appeals to both of you.

Make sure that you offer empathy **not** sympathy. Sympathy is just a way of saying we feel sorry for the other person. It is not a means of reaching a mutually acceptable solution to a problem. Indeed, sympathy often just makes other people feel sorry for themselves.

However empathetic and assertive you are, there will often be times when you face a negative reaction. Here are some useful tips.

❑ *If the other person looks hurt, full of self-pity – tears, even – say something calming: "I'm really sorry to see you like this, shall we talk later?" "I'm sorry that you are taking it so badly but let's see how we can both get something out of this situation."*

❑ *If the other person gets very aggressive, say you understand why they feel so strongly. Keep calm and point out that this isn't getting either of you anywhere. Then present your arguments again. Never retaliate but stand your ground as far as possible.*

❑ *If the other person is grovelling and being over-apologetic, say, firmly, that this kind of behaviour isn't at all constructive.*

Being an assertive customer

❝ *Being in a shop or garage can be very disconcerting for customers. After all, it's our territory, not theirs. I have to admit that there have been times when I deliberately tried to blind the customers with science or make them feel a bit small.* ❞
– Roy Rogers, garage owner

We've all felt intimidated by staff in a restaurant, garage or shop, like Fran Barker from Chapter 2.

> **How easy do you find it to complain about the food or service in a restaurant?**

There are three ways to deal with a restaurant meal that fails to meet the standards you expect:

(1) *Act aggressively* – shout at the waiter and demand your money back.

(2) *Act passively* – which means not acting at all. Smile to the waiter and say "everything's fine" when you actually feel sick.

(3) *Act assertively* – say what you think in a firm but polite manner. Also, if possible, say what you would like to happen. As an example: "I'm sorry to say this meat is very tough and stringy. Could you take it back and bring me something fresher or better cooked?"

As you saw in the last chapter, acting assertively is partly about knowing your rights. It certainly helps to know your rights as a customer. This means doing a bit of research on the local consumer laws. In England and Wales, for instance, customers have the right to be sold goods which correspond to their description, are fit for the purpose sold and of the quality a reasonable person would expect.

Wherever you are, you have the right to be treated fairly, honestly and with courtesy. You also have the right to get what you paid for. If you feel that you are getting an inferior product or service, you have the right to ask for a refund, a replacement or some kind of compensation. You also have the right to be treated with respect and not patronised or looked down upon.

Whether you are entitled in law to refunds, replacements, credit notes or other forms of compensation, will depend on the current state of consumer legislation or the policy of the organisation. The more research you do the stronger your case for compensation should be.

○ Whenever you are in a shop, restaurant, garage etc. think about your rights as a customer.

○ Even if you are not sure about your legal rights, be prepared to defend your moral right to a refund or other form of compensation if things go wrong.

○ Be polite, firm and prepared to listen to the other side's case. But stick to your ground and ask to see a more senior member of staff if necessary

○ Don't be passive or aggressive. When making your case assertively, try to suggest a possible course of action that would be acceptable.

Assertive Talk

❝ *You can learn to respond to other people in an assertive way. When I first started learning to be more assertive, I found that it was easy to say the right thing but when someone came back at me aggressively, I just slumped back to my old, nervous self again – just wishing for a quiet life.* ❞

– Simon Pearson, decorator

While it is important to look assertive – and this comes down to dress and body language – it is even more important to know what to say and how to say it.

Have you ever heard yourself saying one thing but meaning something quite different? A common example could be: "Oh don't worry about me, I really didn't want to go to the cinema anyway." What you really wanted to say was: "I am very upset about being left out of the cinema trip. Next time, please make sure I'm told."

Assertive responses to most situations can be learnt.

Say the right thing, in the right way.

- ❑ *Make sure that you are always treated with justice and fairness. In asking for this, be calm, deliberate and unapologetic. Don't say "I'm really sorry, could I check the bill with you." Instead say "I think this bill might be wrong – I'd be grateful if you could check it with me."*
- ❑ *Express your feelings honestly and frankly. Don't be afraid to have feelings and opinions. They are yours – be comfortable with them.*
- ❑ *Learn to disagree – don't try only to keep the peace. Express your views calmly and honestly.*
- ❑ *If you are given an "unreasonable order" (even from your boss) ask for the reasons. Say that it will be a problem and that you would like to know why it has been issued.*
- ❑ *Don't let some aggressive person dominate the conversation or meeting. Catch the eye of the Chair (if a formal meeting) or get everyone else's attention, and show them how you feel.*
- ❑ *Look people in the eye when you speak to them.*

Ten easy ways to become more assertive

Assertiveness is doing things your way without treading on anybody else's toes.

1. Decide that you want to become more assertive and choose a starting date. Put it in your diary.
2. Pick your top three priorities for becoming more assertive. Think of places (work or home), events (meetings or appraisals), people (your colleagues, your boss, your family).
3. Choose four occasions over the next week or month when you are going to try to be more assertive.
4. Keep telling yourself: you *count*.
5. Practise saying things in an assertive (not aggressive) way. Get straight to the point.
6. Learn to ask for what you want without apologising, simpering or sounding hesitant. It will only be important to the other person if you make it sound as if you mean it.
7. Never take a refusal as a personal attack. Learn to compromise.

8. Think of a second-best or fall-back position if your request is refused.
9. Learn what to say to aggressive or passive people.
10. Respect your own feelings.

There are plenty of ways of starting to become more assertive. Now you know how to begin.

What's in this chapter for you

Conflict isn't so bad
Unbottle your feelings
Stop being your own worst enemy
Criticising others
Taking criticism
Top ways to take and give criticism

> ❝ *In my old, non-assertive days, I used to dread conflict of any kind. I'd do anything to avoid an argument. It was partly because I didn't believe in myself and also because I hated people being unpleasant to each other. Now I see that conflict can, if handled properly, be a good thing.* ❞
> **– Andrea Butler, MD of a publishing company**

Do you try to avoid conflict at all costs? Think honestly about how you behave in awkward situations.

People who try to avoid conflict are often non-assertive, passive types. Similarly, those who always *seek* conflict tend to be overbearing, aggressive people. However, there is a middle ground.

Conflict isn't so bad

Conflict can be creative, provided it is dealt with assertively – and that means no winners, no losers, everyone gains something. Conflict can be a good thing because:

○ *it can stimulate new ideas;*
○ *it can lead to better team work;*
○ *it provides a reason for discussion, debate and analysis;*
○ *it can provide a useful safety valve for all sorts of pent up emotions;*
○ *it keeps people on their toes.*

None of this means that conflict needs to hurt people. Disagreement, yes; but victory at someone else's expense, no.

> ❝ *I used to have a boss that loved stirring things up. He seemed to thrive in an atmosphere of argument, recrimination and tension – the trouble was, no one else did. The rate of staff turnover was high; sickness and absenteeism were rife.* ❞
> **– Andrea Butler**

Conflict can also be fun. A lot depends on how well you know your colleagues or friends. Light-hearted joshing is quite common in the workplace and people don't tend to get upset by it when there is a sense of mutual respect and good feeling. Where there are fierce rivalries and old scores to settle, conflict can be very dangerous.

How to best handle conflicts.

- ❑ *Take control in a conflict situation. Watch out for other people being hurt.*
- ❑ *Never personalise – let debate and discussion flow freely but don't let this become an attack on an individual.*
- ❑ *If you are in the middle of a conflict and very unhappy about it, be honest and say so. Say that there needs to be a different way of resolving the arguments. Challenge others to settle the conflict without resorting to personal abuse or negative attitudes.*
- ❑ *Tell people that conflict which doesn't lead to some kind of improvement for all, is a waste of time, energy and money.*

Unbottle your feelings

> ❝ *There is nothing more destructive than bottling up your feelings. A colleague at work once made me look very foolish in front of my line manager. I've never said anything but I've been harbouring a grudge for years. I still go through endless mental debates: what I should have said or done, what I could still do to get my own back. The trouble is, whenever I see my colleague, I pretend that nothing is wrong.* ❞
> **– Terry Newman, works supervisor**

Bottled-up emotions are harmful. They make us resentful and broody. They keep us awake at night, the injustice of it all gnawing away at our self-confidence.

Does any of this sound familiar?

❑ *You still remember, and resent, a comment that someone made about you years ago.*
❑ *There's something you really want to tell your family but can't face up to it.*
❑ *You want to ask your boss for promotion but you daren't face him or her.*
❑ *You suddenly "snap" and become angry about something that happened days or weeks ago.*
❑ *You often think: "If only I'd said . . . at the time."*

These examples are typical of passive behaviour, although even aggressive people tend to bottle up their emotions at times. Being assertive is about having the self-confidence to express these emotions. There are very good reasons for expressing your feelings:

○ *It makes you feel better – less depressed, less paranoid and less prone to sudden, angry outbursts.*
○ *You can bury an old argument for good.*
○ *You can put the conflict behind you and start to make progress.*
○ *It should lead to better relations with others.*

Bottling up your feelings gets you nowhere. However, it's also true that "letting off steam" can do more harm than good. An angry, uncontrolled response can:

○ *make things worse by upsetting other people;*
○ *make you look foolish;*
○ *make enemies of those on the receiving end;*
○ *prevent you from learning from the situation.*

Handling conflict in an assertive way is neither about bottling up feelings, nor reacting instinctively. It involves taking control of the situation.

If you feel upset by someone's remarks or criticisms, immediately write down your thoughts, taking care to cut out any aggressive or abusive sentiments. This will give you time to cool off and make your response far more emphatic.

Writing things down allows you to see precisely why you feel unjustly treated and you can then edit your comments so they get the point across in the most powerful way. When you are happy with your written response, write it out again as a memo, note or letter. If you prefer, use it as guidance notes for a face-to-face meeting with whomever has upset you.

Do the same for any long-standing grudges. Write a letter saying that you would like to meet again and outlining why you have felt upset for so long.

Stop being your own worst enemy

> ❝ *I always used to blame myself for situations at work. If there was an argument, it was always my fault; if there was a presentation to give, I knew I'd make a mess of it.* ❞
> **– Derek Cowling, sales representative**

Being your own severest critic is a real barrier to assertiveness. How can other people respect you when you don't respect yourself? Passive people are very good at making a crisis out of nothing. They arrive at meetings, interviews, presentations, discussions and so on so wound up that they often make a mess of things. This is "self-fulfilling prophecy" – you're so sure something bad is going to happen that you behave in a way that makes your worst fears come true.

Here are some typical fears that non-assertive people may have at work. How many apply to you?

❑ *I just know that my next interview will go wrong. I'm going to get questions I cannot answer.*
❑ *I'm dreading my next job appraisal – I don't seem to know anything. I'm just not good enough.*

❑ *I'll never get that promotion, the others are so much cleverer or more talented than me.*
❑ *When I face beasty-boss, I know I'll turn to jelly.*
❑ *There's bound to be a big row there – I'm really dreading it.*
❑ *I'm bound to make mistakes with this next job, and it's got to be 100 per cent correct.*

Negative attitudes such as these are a common feature of passive people. They are caused by:

○ *feelings of inadequacy;*
○ *thinking the worst will happen;*
○ *wanting to avoid conflict;*
○ *setting unrealistic goals.*

These negative feelings can best be tackled in three simple ways:

(1) Banish negative thoughts and work out (on paper if necessary) a strategy for being and sounding positive.
(2) Never set your goals beyond reach – choose objectives that you *can* meet.
(3) Challenge your own inner voice on each negative point. Tell yourself what you *can* do, not what you can't.

❝ *It was a deal-clinching presentation. I was dreading it so I'd planned something to rival the opening ceremony for the Olympics. My worst fears came to pass – as I nervously leapt around the stage trying to use all the equipment I'd brought, I knocked over my slide projector and smashed it. My presentation went downhill from there, to say the least, and I lost the contract.* ❞
– Derek Cowling

Look back at meetings, projects etc. that you feel have gone badly for you. What you need to ask yourself is: "Am I exaggerating the significance of this?" – it's very easy to do.

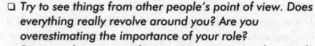

Put things in perspective.

- *Try to see things from other people's point of view. Does everything really revolve around you? Are you overestimating the importance of your role?*
- *Downgrade any unrealistic expectations – maybe you don't have to get everything right first time, or perhaps the expected costs of making mistakes are not so high.*
- *Work out a strategy for dealing with awkward questions you cannot answer, and unreasonable requests. The best tactic is to be honest and say: "I can't really deal with that now but, if you'll give me time, I'll get back to you."*
- *Challenge every self-doubting question that springs to mind. Is this really the case, or am I underestimating myself?*

A true picture of what you're worth is invaluable in developing assertiveness skills.

Criticising others

❝ *One of the most difficult aspects of my job is criticising my staff. I hate doing it and sometimes lie awake the whole night before working out what I'm going to say - and how I'm going to say it.* ❞
– Frank Baker, personnel director

It is (or can be) very difficult for a non-assertive person to criticise others. The reasons are:

○ *fear of upsetting people;*
○ *fear of an angry reaction:*
○ *fear of being wrong.*

The essential point about criticising other people is that you should be targeting their *behaviour*, not them as people. This section could have been called "Criticising other people's behaviour".

How do you feel when someone criticises your work or behaviour? Well, do as you would be done by.

Criticism is often an essential fact of life. If you honestly feel that a job or task falls below expectations, then you should say so. Never bottle up criticism.

The art of assertiveness is to know how to criticise behaviour without making it a personal attack. Criticism should never:

○ *belittle the person, making them feel upset or inadequate;*
○ *cause a heated argument or lead to a fight;*
○ *be used just to get things off your chest;*
○ *become a management style ("having a go at my staff keeps them on their toes!").*

The role of criticism is to make things better – to put things back on course to success. If criticising someone doesn't lead to an improvement, then it is not worth doing. Criticism is a very risky business. As we've already seen, people can bottle up old grievances and perceived slights for many years. This isn't to say that criticism should never be used. It is an essential tool of progress, if used correctly.

Tips on criticising constructively.

❑ *Criticism of others should always be positive. Always say what can be done to improve next time.*
❑ *Never criticise others when you are feeling angry – wait until you have calmed down and work out how to make progress.*
❑ *Choose the right place and time.*
❑ *Always maintain your composure, stay in control, and be honest about how you feel.*
❑ *Give the other person an opportunity to have a say.*
❑ *Steer away from assigning blame – it's non-productive and will not resolve the problem.*
❑ *Get the situation into perspective – was the mistake really so important?*
❑ *Be prepared for the other person getting upset – don't continue until they feel composed.*
❑ *Ask the other person for their views on how to improve the situation.*
❑ *Follow up any criticism with a summary of what has been decided.*
❑ *End on a friendly or, at least, non-aggressive note.*

Taking criticism

❝ *Even as a mature adult, I find it hard to cope with criticism. However justified it is, or thoughtfully presented, I can't help feeling it's a personal attack.* ❞

– Frank Baker

How do you respond to being criticised?

❑ I feel guilty.
❑ I defend my position whatever.
❑ It really upsets me.
❑ I'd do anything to avoid it.
❑ I like a good argument.
❑ No one would dare!

These are all either passive or aggressive responses. The assertive way to receive criticism is:

○ to accept that the other person has the right to criticise your actions;
○ not to accept that the other person has the right to criticise you as a person;
○ to accept constructive criticism and see it as a learning experience;
○ not to accept insults or abuse but to stand your ground calmly and honestly.

Remember:

❑ *Try to welcome criticism as part of your personal development.*
❑ *Always insist that you have a say in working out what happens as a result of the criticism.*
❑ *If the other person gets abusive or angry, say: "I'm sorry but this sounds more like abuse than genuine criticism."*
❑ *Do not tolerate any kind of personal attack. Say that you do not think it necessary, appropriate or in any way constructive.*
❑ *Be prepared to give your own side of the story. If necessary ask for a chance to give your version of events.*
❑ *Don't let others make vague criticisms – ask for specific examples.*

> ❑ *Check your body language as you are being criticised – sit up, or stand very straight and look the person in the eye (but not aggressively). Don't shuffle but maintain the calm pose of a person in control. If necessary, make notes or ask for an arbitrator to be at the meeting.*

If you suspect that you are heading for some kind of conflict – for instance, if you or your department has been involved in a blunder – avoid being "hijacked" by someone who has had plenty of time to prepare the criticism. Be ready to ask for time to prepare your response so you can discuss the matter on an equal footing.

Top ways to take and give criticism

Criticism should be a constructive process.

1. Tell yourself that some conflict can be a very good thing – don't always try to avoid it.
2. Take control in any situation where there is conflict or criticism. Don't be passive or aggressive.
3. Never tolerate personal abuse. Criticism should only ever be levelled at behaviour.
4. Criticism that doesn't lead to some kind of improvement is not worth having. Point this out to people who are simply on the offensive.
5. Write down your feelings if you would rather not confront someone face to face. This also allows you to edit your comments and present your point more convincingly.
6. Criticise others in a positive way, giving feedback only on behaviour. Give the other person a chance to contribute.
7. Avoid blame – it won't make things better.
8. Receive criticism as a learning experience, don't take it personally.
9. If you are not being criticised usefully, ask for specific examples of where and how you went wrong, and what should have been done.
10. Insist on being criticised at a time that suits all parties. Make sure you prepare for the session.

Remember that criticism should not stoop to personal attack or abuse. The latter is always negative and just leads to long-term grudges and upset. Positive criticism is actually essential in any organisation that wants to move ahead. Welcome criticism and be prepared for it.

What's in this chapter for you

Stop saying "yes" when you mean "no"
Using assertiveness to say "no"
Start with yourself
Saying "no" to the boss
Top tips for saying "no"

❝ *I've always found it hard to say "no" – especially when friends or work colleagues ask a favour. It must be the way I was brought up. I thought it really rude to let someone down. What I didn't realise was how much of my time I was giving up to please others.* ❞
– Gavin Jenkins, catering manager

Why do we often say "yes" to something that we would rather not do? If you are prone to this, you'll know how frustrating it can be. But you *can* learn to say "no".

Stop saying "yes" when you mean "no"

Do you find it difficult to say "no", even to a friend? Here are some typical situations:

- ○ *A good friend wants to visit but you are very busy.*
- ○ *A neighbour wants to borrow your lawnmower but you have planned to use it.*
- ○ *The family wants to go out, but you want to stay in.*
- ○ *A beggar asks you for money.*
- ○ *A door-to-door salesman tries to appeal to your sympathy.*
- ○ *A woman asks you for a charitable contribution in the street.*
- ○ *A colleague at work asks you to cover for his or her absence.*

How do you react in these situations? Can you say "no"? Don't worry if you can't, you're not alone, and you can overcome the problem.

Why is saying "no" so difficult for some people? The answer is they see it as letting someone down or appearing to be rude. When you say "no", how do you feel?

○ *"Other people will get annoyed with me."*
○ *"I'd be letting them down."*
○ *"I am being rude or selfish."*
○ *"I'm getting rather 'above' myself."*
○ *"I'll find it more difficult to ask them for a favour in future."*
○ *"I will be unpopular."*

Saying "yes" when you mean "no" is a typical symptom of passive behaviour. It means ignoring your own views and wishes in order to meet someone else's objectives.

What are the consequences of passively saying "yes"?

❑ *You get a reputation for being a "doormat".*
❑ *You become overworked and stressed.*
❑ *You'll harbour hidden resentments about the people who have asked you to do things.*
❑ *You may eventually lose your temper and control, which will only make things worse.*
❑ *You'll be tempted to become more aggressive and this is as destructive as being passive.*

❝ *Once people know that you always agree to any request, you'll find yourself being exploited and overworked. It's as if your time isn't as valuable as theirs.* ❞
– Gavin Jenkins

You may, of course, be the type of person who acts aggressively whenever a favour is asked. Does any of this sound familiar?

○ *"I'm well known for saying 'no' to requests, so people are usually too scared to ask."*
○ *"I don't like giving the impression of being exploitable, so I turn down requests whenever I can."*
○ *"If anyone asks me a favour, or for money, I tell them in no uncertain terms to go away and stop bothering me."*

These are all aggressive responses. They take little or no account of the other person's feelings. It's an "I win, you lose" situation.

Using assertiveness to say "no"

It is perfectly possible to learn to refuse requests in an assertive manner – in other words to respect your own wishes without having to score a victory over someone else. The three key principles throughout this chapter are:

(1) Honesty – with others and, even more importantly, with yourself. Give reasons why you can't do something, not excuses.

(2) Self-respect – your rights are just as important as the other person's. You have a right to say "no".

(3) Communication – being able to *share* with the other person the reason why you have to turn down a request.

To respond assertively, begin by trying to buy yourself some thinking time. Say "I'll have to think about that." Never sound apologetic and remember, you have the right to refuse requests. You must believe, too, that you *can* learn how to say "no" effectively.

Learn to replace your fears with assertive thinking:

❑ *If you feel "people will get annoyed", think "they should respect my feelings".*

❑ *If you feel "people will be let down", remember it shouldn't be a "you win, I lose" situation.*

❑ *"I'm being rude": it isn't rude to express your point of view, it just depends how you say it.*

❑ *If you feel "I'm not important enough to say it", remember that you are just as important as the others.*

❑ *If you're worried about asking for favours in future, bear in mind that, if there is mutual respect and you have been honest and direct in saying "no", then things shouldn't degenerate into a question of tit for tat.*

Think of a request as an opening round in a negotiation. There are various options:

○ *"I can do some of the job now, and the rest later."*
○ *"If you can help me with it, I'll do it."*
○ *"If you do blah-blah-blah for me in exchange, I'd be glad to help."*

○ *"I can't do it, but I'll help you find someone who can."*
○ *"I can't help but let's work out together how the task or job can be done."*

Always be honest and think how you can help the other person while still saying "no". Remember, you should be striving for a "you win, I win" result.

Start with yourself

❝ *I believe that one of the keys to assertiveness is an ability to value your own time as much as anyone else's. It's much easier to say 'no' if you are really convinced of the reasons why you can't do it. It's got to start with you.* ❞
– Gwen Littlewood, assertiveness trainer

How do you value your time? It's a precious commodity so you shouldn't squander it on things you don't want to do.

Self-respect is the key to assertiveness. It is also important to be totally honest with yourself. If you are honest with yourself, you can be truly honest with others and explain the real reasons (not excuses) why you have to turn down a request.

Saying "no" is not a rude thing to do. We are brought up to be polite and caring but this does not mean that we have to be at everyone's beck and call.

Here are a couple of useful exercises that will get you geared up for saying "no" assertively.

☐ *Practise in front of a mirror – say "no" without saying "no, sorry". Try to say it in a polite, friendly manner. Smile, and mean it.*
☐ *Practise saying "no, and the reason is . . .". Make sure the reason is genuine and comes over that way.*

Get used to using the following genuine reasons for saying no:

○ *"I have too many other jobs to do."*
○ *"This would have to take a very low priority at the moment."*
○ *"I don't think I'm the best person for this job"* (and mean it if you say it).
○ *"I'm under a lot of pressure at the moment."*
○ *"I really don't want to let you down or do a substandard job, so I must say no."*

> **❝** *Saying 'no' isn't just about using a two-letter word. It's very important to know how to say it without offending or putting someone else down. And, even more importantly, you have to know why you've said it.* **❞**
> – **Gwen Littlewood**

There are some dos and dont's that you should always keep in mind when delivering a refusal. When you say "no":

○ *Don't say it an apologetic, timid voice – say "no", not "sorry, but no".*
○ *Show with your body language that it's OK for you to refuse. Stand tall, chin up; talk in a calm, measured way; look the other person straight in the eye.*
○ *Don't sound guilty or hesitant. If you say "er, well, the fact is . . . I mean . . . no", it sounds as if you could be persuaded to accept.*
○ *Give reasons and try to help the other person find a solution.*

Here are a couple of ways of launching the new assertive you.

❑ *Start with the easier situations: say "no" to good friends or family over relatively unimportant tasks. Gradually build up from there.*
❑ *Carry a diary with you and use it every day. If you really don't have time to do a job, refer to the diary and tell the other person why you have to refuse a request. Try something like: "Let's see, I've got to finish the report by the 12th, there's a family function on the 13th and next week it looks like I'm tied up in meetings. So, as you can see, the answer will have to be 'no'."*

Saying "no" to the boss

❝ *It's never easy to do this. You always feel that saying 'no' may well jeopardise your chances of promotion. However, as the MD of a medium-sized company, I can assure you that I much prefer honesty. I also prefer an employee to tell me that a job can't be done properly rather than having to accept second best. I'm honest with my staff, and I want them to be honest with me.* ❞
– Linda Barnes, MD of a printing firm

Assuming that you have a boss, do you find it hard to say "no" to him or her? Again, the first step is to ask yourself why and come up with honest answers.

A huge number of employees quake in their shoes at the thought of having to refuse their boss' requests. Common reasons given for this are:

○ *"I might lose my job."*
○ *"I might lose his or her trust."*
○ *"I'm just too scared to say it."*
○ *"Surely it's my job to do whatever I'm asked to do."*

These are all passive, or non-assertive responses. They all show a lack of self-respect or sense of worth. It's time to face up to your fears and realise that there are many compelling reasons for starting to manage your boss more effectively – and that means learning to say "no" now and again.

After all, when you think about it, it's in your boss' interests to:

○ *make sure you stay fit and well – asking you to do too much can damage your health;*
○ *keep you employed (assuming, of course, that you're doing the job competently);*
○ *know what you really think – how else can he or she make the right decisions?*
○ *treat all employees well so as to get the best from them.*

Here are two things to try if you've got the boss from hell.

❑ *Put your refusal in writing but ask for a follow-up meeting if further explanation is required.*
❑ *Ask for time to consider the request and, in the meantime, send a short summary of all the other work you have to do.*

> ❝ *I'm often really surprised at how much a member of staff has to do at any one time. I respect staff who say to me: 'No, I can't do this because I'm still trying to meet deadlines A, B, and C'.* ❞
> **– Linda Barnes**

Using the assertive techniques we've looked at so far – confident body language, a firm but conciliatory tone, a willingness to explore other ways of getting the job done – saying "no" will not mean that you are seen as a trouble-maker. You will be respected for presenting your own case in a clear, calm but committed way. If you must say "yes", ask how to put other current tasks into an order of priority.

Top tips for saying "no"

If you say "no" in an assertive way (without being passive or aggressive), you'll find it easy to refuse things you don't want to do.

1. Buy yourself some thinking time. Ask for fuller details before saying "yes". Ask how long the task will take, who will help you, what exactly needs to be done and so on.
2. Use positive body language when refusing – this means appearing relaxed, calm and deliberate in your delivery.
3. Give an honest reason why you can't say "yes" but not an excuse. Don't invent a reason – if you don't believe it, neither will the other person.
4. Remind yourself that your time is just as valuable as that of the person asking the favour.

5. Start small – practise assertive responses with close friends or with the family. Move on to colleagues or subordinates at work, and then on to your managers, customers, and so on.
6. Never be aggressive when saying "no" – say it with a smile and a concern to help the other person where you can.
7. Carry a diary and refer to it to show why you don't have the time to say "yes". Don't be afraid to include all the things that you think are important – birthdays, dental appointments, holidays, family visits etc.
8. Keep your explanations short. Never ramble. The more you speak, the less convincing you will be to yourself and the other person.
9. Practise saying "no" in the mirror – learn to look resolute yet friendly and concerned. And get out of the habit of saying "no, sorry" instead of "no".

With these techniques, you will soon be able to say "no", and communicate that you mean it.

What's in this chapter for you

Dealing with aggressive colleagues and customers
Dealing with passive people
Being more assertive at meetings
Assertive body language
Ten ways to develop a new you at work

This chapter shows you how to hone your assertiveness skills and use them effectively at work.

> Do you ever feel that your voice isn't heard or that you don't seem to make the impact you should do at work? Does it always seem to be you that's left juggling the work pressures and your personal life? If so, it's time to change.

Dealing with aggressive colleagues and customers

> *" I've always hated those situations when someone would come at you really aggressively. Despite all my assertiveness training, I still find it tough facing up to someone who is really angry or rude. Maybe I'll never change; perhaps it's ingrained in my personality. "*

This quote from a well-respected and successful entrepreneur seems worryingly familiar. Many of us find it really difficult to face up to aggressive people and prefer a quiet life. But, in truth, aggressiveness on the part of others means only that there is a lack of mutual respect. A person who gets away with being aggressive has "victims" who are passive receivers. This is destructive and unnecessary. You can learn to develop very effective defences against aggression.

The first thing to remember is that an aggressive person can only succeed if you let him or her get the better of you or upset you. Learn to avoid some of the immediate responses to aggression such as:

- ❑ feeling hurt and upset;
- ❑ feeling angry and ready to hit back;
- ❑ feeling scared and ready to do whatever the other person tells you;
- ❑ pretending to be unscathed but actually feeling either guilty or small (or both).

Any self-deprecating response plays right into the hands of an aggressive person. It gives them the upper hand and lets them manipulate you into doing what they want (as well as making you look foolish).

What form does aggression take? Be on the look out for:

- ○ personal abuse or attack;
- ○ people trying to make you look small in the eyes of others;
- ○ people who dismiss your contribution or make sarcastic comments about your work or you;
- ○ people using threats to get their own way.

❝ We used to have a colleague who always tried to get his own way by threatening to resign if we didn't do what he wanted. Eventually we called his bluff – after feeling rather sorry for himself, he soon changed his ways. ❞

– **Rob Lee, design consultant**

How do you feel when people are being aggressive towards you in any of the ways we've outlined? How do you normally react? Think of a time when you really wished you'd handled an aggressive person in a better way. What should you have done (apart from resorting to the telescopic baseball bat in your briefcase!)?

Common reactions to aggression are:

- guilt;
- anger;
- the feeling of having made a fool of yourself;
- a determination to do better next time.

As always, you need to overcome your negative feelings, or at least keep them hidden, and keep your composure. What's needed is a way of reacting to an aggressive person without being either passive or aggressive. You can do this by responding assertively.

Here are some assertive tactics to use when faced with an aggressive person.

- ❏ Change the location. If the person is on his or her "home ground" in the office, factory floor, or shop etc., move into "neutral territory" or even better rearrange the meeting on your patch. Neutral territory could be a meeting room, the corridor or any other quiet spot. It's important to make sure it's well away from any of the aggressor's supporters or henchmen (so that he or she can't "play to the gallery").
- ❏ Try to quieten the angry person down. You will sound and look more professional and in control if you deal with every angry outburst in a calming way. Sometimes it's a good idea to let the other person get all the anger out before saying anything.
- ❏ Maintain eye contact as you listen to the tirade, and maintain assertive body language.
- ❏ Remember that you are trying to achieve a "win-win" situation. Recognise their feelings and show that you care. Try: "Yes, I can see that you really upset by this, I hope you'll let me give my side of the story" or "I can understand your anger, now let's work out what we're going to do to put things right."
- ❏ Ask lots of "open" questions to clarify the situation as the aggressive person sees it. Avoid answering back with counter-accusations.

Open questions are those that cannot easily be answered with a
"yes" or "no". They usually start with: what, where, why, how,
when, who?

> **❝** *If anyone bursts into my office sounding angry or abusive, I
> always get them to sit down, allow them some time to let off steam
> and then, before I give my response, fire a lot of questions at them to
> clarify the situation – things like: 'Who told you this?' or 'When did
> this happen?' or 'What did you do next?'.* **❞**
> **– Bea Fernhill, financial controller**

Asking open questions not only buys some time for you to think
but also tends to take the sting out of the situation. It is important
that you listen to the answers given with empathy and with keen
interest (it will only upset them more if you appear to be
indifferent or cynical).

When dealing with aggression:

❑ *Always stand your ground and say what you have to say. If
you can't think of an instant reply, buy some thinking time –
say something like: "Thanks for telling me these things. I
need a little time to think about what you've said. I'll get
back to you."*

❑ *If you are confident of your position, state your case calmly
and without recriminations. You will be in a stronger
position if you haven't interrupted the aggressive person too
often and you wait for the right time to reply.*

❑ *If all else fails, be totally honest about your feelings and
insist on another meeting at a mutually acceptable time,
perhaps in the presence of other interested parties (your
boss or a lawyer, for instance). Alternatively, you could ask
the aggressor to put everything in writing to clarify the
matter and create a record of his or her grievance.*

> **❝** *If I'm really going nowhere fast with an angry colleague or
> customer, I usually say: 'Look, what you are saying is rather
> upsetting and very unfair. I would like some time to consider my
> point of view – when can we meet again?'.* **❞**
> **– Bea Fernhill**

Dealing with passive people

Passive people can often get their own way by appealing to your sense of loyalty, humanity, friendship or "better nature". They can be incredibly manipulative in their own way. Beware emotional blackmail – it's there to sap your assertiveness.

> **"** *Dealing with my old headmaster was impossible – it was like nailing jelly to a wall. You never seemed to get anywhere except into a downward spiral of grovelling apologies. He made you feel really guilty for upsetting him. That's how he always got his own way in staff meetings.* **"**
> **– Jack Peters, former teacher**

Watch out for passive behaviour. People with this type of personality tend to:

○ *hide their true feelings;*
○ *tell you one thing but do another;*
○ *be quick with excuses why things can't be done your way;*
○ *moan, groan and blame fate for their sorry lot;*
○ *constantly look for approval;*
○ *make frequent self-deprecating comments ("I knew I'd make a mess of it");*
○ *try to flatter you at their own expense.*

It is very difficult to have an adult, two-way "win-win" relationship with someone who is always putting themselves down or excusing their own perceived shortcomings.

Here are some ideas on dealing with passive types.

❑ *Try to pin them down. Get them to explain their position with lots of open questions. This usually works well: "What makes you think you can't do it?" or "What's the best way to make progress here?"*
❑ *Get them to tell you what they really think. Try: "I think there's something else on your mind, I'd like to know what it is."*
❑ *Don't fall for their self-deprecation. Challenge their self-image. A word of encouragement might be all they need.*
❑ *Encourage them to go on an assertiveness course. Or, get them to buy this book – it'll do wonders for their self-confidence!*

Being more assertive at meetings

❝ The business meeting can be a showcase of egos. It is the perfect place for showing off, throwing weight about, or cowering in corners. It's the ideal place to practise becoming more assertive. ❞
– Miles Swinton, management consultant

It's true that business meetings are situations in which many people want to be more assertive.

How often have you come away from a business meeting feeling that:

❑ *you didn't say enough?*
❑ *you let all sorts of decisions go ahead without a murmer?*
❑ *you were bullied and railroaded by an aggressive individual?*
❑ *you sounded too apologetic and failed to make your point?*
❑ *you got angry and embarrassed all present?*
❑ *you felt totally detached from it all?*

The thought of being assertive at meetings can be scary. It is a formal occasion where colleagues, perhaps rivals, are there to judge your performance, and vice versa. Your professional opinion and judgement are being sought and it's a chance to shine. The stakes are often high. Meetings can be tense situations where it feels almost impossible to be assertive.

Yet there are some things in your favour. Meetings are usually fairly formal, with predictable rules of behaviour. For instance, it is often the case that everyone must speak through the chair, and there is a set agenda which is available in advance. This allows you to prepare what you want to say carefully, and how and when you want to say it.

If you want to appear more assertive, try out these tips when you next have a meeting.

- *Prepare thoroughly your case on certain issues. Don't worry if no one else agrees with you at first – if you sound confident, they may come round.*
- *Make at least one positive contribution to the meeting, even if you agree with everything that's been said and don't really have anything to add. Be an assertive agree-er: "I must say that everything I've heard so far convinces me that this is the right course." This is active (rather than passive) agreement and will be much more respected as such.*
- *Ask for clarification if anything seems unclear. It is a good sign that you are listening to the arguments and still engaged in the debate.*
- *Remember that if you've been invited to join a meeting, you have equal rights to be heard, seen and respected.*
- *Insist on being heard without interruption. (This is where you can call on the formal rules of business meetings to serve your purpose. Think of the chair as a kind of referee – appeal, if necessary, to the chair's authority.)*
- *Don't sit there passively accepting things you don't really understand or agree with. You could always say: "Look, I'm not happy with this – can we have time to consider our views in more depth?" or "I'd like to be honest and say that I don't really understand this: does anyone else feel this way?" (chances are that others will suddenly emerge to support your position).*
- *Try to sound calm and always in control. If anything makes you angry, take some slow deep breaths and talk only when you feel more at ease. Aggressive behaviour will get you nowhere.*
- *If it seems you are being ignored, ask the others at the meeting for their reaction to your ideas. For example: "I've not had much reaction to my idea and I wonder what, for instance, Gill thinks about it?"*
- *Don't accept others dismissing your views. Ask for a reason.*

A useful strategy to use before a meeting is to play the politician. Canvas views from others who will be attending and try to build some alliances. If you have ideas, circulate them beforehand to people you can trust. Tell them that this will be brought up at the meeting and you would like their support.

Assertive body language

> 66 *Assertiveness is often more about how we say something than what we say. This is where body language is so important. It is how you are going to be judged. If your lips say 'This is what I think' but your body says 'I'm really unsure about this', then other people will have doubts about your sincerity.* 99
> **– Miles Swinton**

Assertive body language is a vital part of getting your message across. This is not to say that body language is enough on its own – your message has to be solid, too.

Assuming that you have confidence in your message, how do you make sure that your body language says the same thing? Think of people who have impressed you in meetings and try to identify the posture and delivery style they adopted.

The way you hold yourself will speak volumes about you. Adopt an assertive posture when you speak:

○ whether you're standing or sitting, keep your spine straight and lengthened;
○ keep your head still and face the other person;
○ maintain eye contact but don't turn it into a staring contest – give the other person a break every now and then;
○ keep your hands relaxed and don't fidget;
○ if you "dry up" just stop (take a drink or a breath) and start again when you are ready.

Avoid postures that make you look as if you don't respect your own views. For instance, your hands can give you away if you are nervous or uncertain about what you are saying. Here are some actions to avoid:

○ constantly wiping or wringing your hands;
○ nervously tapping your teeth with a pencil;
○ grasping your knees with both hands or hugging yourself;
○ sitting or standing too far away or too close up;
○ nervous giggling or scratching.

Mastering body language is all to do with self-observation. Here are a couple of ideas to help you practise.

❑ *Watch out for your hand gestures. You may have got into the habit of constantly flicking your hair, twiddling a pencil, juggling sugar cubes, doodling or doing a bit of origami during meetings. These are not things assertive, confident people do so work at stamping the habit out.*
❑ *Get a friend to watch or video you in conversation with a colleague or stranger. Analyse your body language: is it advertising that you are nervous, shy, aggressive, unsure, uncomfortable? Once you know what you are doing wrong, you can practise overcoming your problem.*

Wear clothes that are comfortable and make you feel confident. Never wear new shoes or unfamiliar styles for the first time at an important meeting – it can crack your veneer of assertiveness if you feet are creaking and the others are blinded by your loud new jacket. And, try to smile, but don't overdo it – this isn't a beauty contest.

Ten ways to develop a new you at work

Being assertive in the workplace can radically improve the quality of your life. Follow these tips and see for yourself.

1. If you are confronted by an aggressive person, take them to a neutral location to continue the discussion. Suggest putting the grievance down on paper. Buy thinking time however you can.
2. Acknowledge an angry or aggressive person's attitude and, when they are ready to listen to you, ask them to hear your viewpoint.
3. Keep calm and in control. Always tell yourself: "My views are equally important and it's in both our interests for me to be heard."
4. Tell non-assertive people that you would like to know what they are really thinking. Be calm, helpful and understanding – make it easier for them to tell you what's really going on.

5. Never go into a meeting unprepared – do your homework and decide what, when and where you will speak. Try to build alliances before the meeting.

6. If you don't understand something, ask for clarification – and don't apologise or grovel.

7. Work on developing an assertive posture – always stand or sit up straight, use eye contact and don't fidget.

8. Develop an assertive voice – measured, unhurried, and without hesitation. You can practise this by rehearsing things you want to say in front of a mirror. The trick is to exude confidence.

9. Get a friend to observe you talking to others (preferably in a work situation). Iron out all the little tell-tale, non-assertive gestures.

10. Choose appropriate clothes in which you feel comfortable and confident. (An important business meeting is not the place to unveil your latest designer bondage pants!).

Now that you have read through this book and tried out some of the great tips, you should be well on the way to becoming a much more assertive you. Enjoy your new-found status as a self-respecting person. There's no better time than now to start being more assertive. Do you think the world is ready for the new you?